MW00779579

THE CALIFORNIA GOLD RUSH

by Deborah Bruss

MODERN CURRICULUM PRESS
Pearson Learning Group

James Marshall

In January 1848, James Marshall stood by a river in California. He was building a mill for a man named John Sutter. Marshall saw a shiny yellow stone under the water. It was no bigger than a dime. He wondered if it was real gold. Or was it only fool's gold? They both glitter.

Marshall knew how to identify gold. Fool's gold is hard. Softness indicates real gold. He bit the nugget. His teeth left marks. This was the first test.

Then Marshall hammered it flat with a rock. Fool's gold would break, but this did not. Both tests seemed to indicate that this was real!

Marshall tried one more test. He put the nugget into a boiling pot. In the pot was lye, a strong chemical used to wash clothes. It would mark fool's gold. When Marshall pulled out the nugget it was unharmed. This final test proved it. He had found real gold!

Marshall galloped down to Sutter's fort and burst into Mr. Sutter's office. But Sutter was not happy with the news. He knew that if word got out, many people would come. They would tear up the riverbanks and overrun his farm looking for more gold. Sutter asked his workers to keep the gold a secret.

Not many people paid attention to the gold, until a man named Sam Brannon went to the small town of San Francisco. He walked up and down the streets with a bottle of gold dust.

San Francisco in the mid-1800s

"Gold!" he shouted. "Gold from the American River." Brannon had a selfish reason to tell about the gold. He wanted miners to come to his store to buy tools.

Soon most of the people left town and hurried up the river. Teachers, tailors, doctors, and even the sheriff hoped to strike it rich. Most of Sutter's workers also left him. Crops rotted in the fields. Miners tore down Sutter's mill. They used the wood for their camps.

Finding the gold took a bit of work. If you were panning for gold in 1850, you'd first scoop up sand and water in your pan. Then you'd swirl it around and around. Sand, which weighs less than gold, would slosh over the side. The heavier gold would stay on the bottom of the pan. You might see little nuggets of it shining right up at you.

Thousands of people caught "gold fever." Many of them left for California in 1849, so they were called "forty-niners." They came from all over the world.

Most forty-niners were unmarried men. But the record indicates that a few women did come along. The miners had to leave almost everything back home. There was no room to carry such household items as furniture, dishes, jewelry, and clothes.

There were three main routes to get to California from the East. Some forty-niners traveled over land on the Oregon-California Trail. Others traveled on sailing ships around the southern tip of South America. And some sailed down to Panama, hiked through the jungle to the Pacific Ocean, and then sailed up the coast to California.

About half the forty-niners traveled the first route—over land. They usually traveled by wagon. Most of them did not realize how difficult the journey would be. They struggled to cross prairies, mountains, and deserts. Many people got sick and died from drinking dirty water. Some died from having no water at all.

The second route—sailing around the rocky tip of South America—took at least five months, if things went well. But things often did not go well. Some of the most dangerous waters in the world lie at the tip of South America. Dangerous storms are common, and sometimes the storms rage for days. Other times, there is no wind at all for days. Back then, ships had to wait for the wind to come up again. There was little to do but look at the sapphire-blue water.

The third route was faster, but it meant taking a boat to Panama first. Then the forty-niners hiked through dense rainforests to the Pacific Ocean. There were many dangerous snakes and insects there. Many people died from terrible tropical diseases.

Miners found no rest once they reached California. Day after day they shoveled, sifted, and washed the gravel. Sometimes a miner would strike it rich. In one month he or she might find thousands of dollars' worth of gold.

But most miners were not lucky. One bucket of dirt might only give ten cents' worth of gold. A miner washing 160 buckets in one day could earn sixteen dollars. That was a lot of money at that time in most places, but not in California. No one got rich on sixteen dollars a day.

For the first time, many women had a chance to earn money. A few became miners like the men. Most cooked, ran boarding houses, and washed clothes.

Many people earned money by selling things to the miners. Levi Strauss was one of them. He came to California to sell canvas for tents. He noticed that the miners' pants wore out quickly, so he made stronger ones from denim. He went on to make his fortune selling jeans.

By 1850, most of California's "easy" gold was gone. Still, more people kept coming. Most of the gold now lay underground. High-powered hoses blasted away the dirt and rocks. Miners dug mines. Dangerous holes dotted the landscape, and underground mines collapsed.

Over 100,000 people came to California during the Gold Rush. A few of them struck it rich. But many more died from diseases and accidents. At least ten thousand lost their lives. Many Native Americans lost their lives and their land. The land and people of California would never look the same again.

In 1847 only eight hundred people lived in San Francisco. After the world heard about the promise of gold there, the city grew quickly. Within three years 25,000 people called the city home.

San Francisco before the Gold Rush

Modern-day San Francisco

For thousands of years people have searched for treasures that lay hidden underground. Gold is just one of these. People have also mined silver and tin, diamonds, and sapphires. They sold their finds for money. Or they made jewelry, decorations, and tools.

Only gold has created such a frantic rush by so many people. And it all started in California in 1848, when one man found a few small nuggets in the American River.

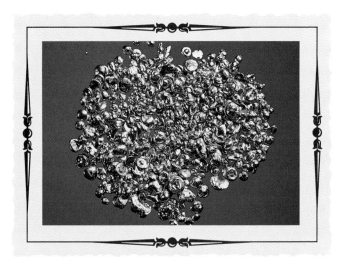